PULL

The Magnetism Files

Discovery Channel School
Science Collections

© 1999 by Discovery Communications, Inc. All rights reserved under International and Pan-American Copyright Conventions.
No part of this book may be reproduced in any form or by any electronic or mechanical means, including
information storage devices or systems, without prior written permission from the publisher.
For information regarding permission, write to Discovery Channel School, 7700 Wisconsin Avenue, Bethesda, MD 20814.
Printed in the USA ISBN: 1-56331-910-1

1 2 3 4 5 6 7 8 9 10 PO 06 05 04 03 02 00 99

Discovery Communications, Inc., produces high-quality television programming
interactive media, books, films, and consumer products. Discovery Networks, a division of Discovery
Communications Inc., operates and manages Discovery Channel, TLC, Animal Planet, Discovery Health Channel, and Travel Channel.

CONTENTS

PULL

Stuck on You

Have you ever explored your house with a small magnet and tested to see what it would pick up? You could play with the magnet for hours, but what you would learn is similar to what people of long ago found true of magnetism: you can see its effects, but not how it works.

In this book, Discovery Channel takes you on a voyage through space and time to discover how the mystery of magnetism was solved. You'll also see that magnetism is responsible for more than just keeping your grocery list stuck to the refrigerator door. In fact, magnetism goes beyond modern technology. It works its magic on common items you would never imagine and can be considered essential to life itself.

The Magnetism Files

Why is this pigeon wearing a silly hat? See page 26.

Final Project

Magnetism

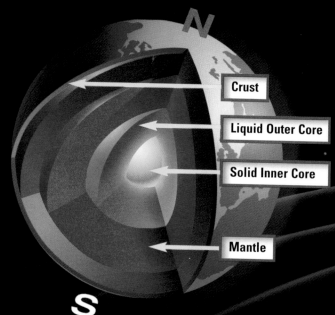

Crust

Liquid Outer Core

Solid Inner Core

Mantle

N

S

Have you ever felt the push or pull between two magnets? You may already know that every magnet has a north pole and a south pole, and opposite poles attract while similar poles repel. But do you know why? It's all because of magnetism, which, like gravity, is part of one of the fundamental forces of nature. Unlike gravity, magnetism does not show up equally in all types of matter. It most often occurs in substances containing the elements such as iron, nickel, and cobalt, and it gets its start right at the heart of the matter—in the very atoms that make up those elements.

Even though you can't see them, all atoms are in constant motion and they're composed of different parts. At their center, in the nucleus, atoms have particles called protons and neutrons. Moving around the outside of atoms are tiny negatively charged particles called electrons, which, as their name suggests, are also involved in electricity. These electrons don't just move around the nucleus of the atom. They spin as well. While spinning, they create a tiny electric current that creates a small magnetic field around each and every electron. A magnetic field is an invisible area around an object which can interact with the magnetic field around another object.

Because of the forces of attraction and repulsion, different atoms of a substance align their magnetic fields with each other to create larger magnetized regions called domains. In most materials, these magnetic domains are randomly organized so that their north and south poles don't line up with each other. As a result, the material is not magnetic. However, in materials containing elements like iron, cobalt and nickel, the different magnetic domains have the ability to line up. If enough of them line up, you've got a magnet. So, the bottom line is that the magnets on your refrigerator stick because of the spin of electrons in their atoms!

Magnetic Field—any field that surrounds a magnet. For Earth, the surrounding area of space affected by Earth's magnetism.

Solar Winds—high energy particles that are ejected from the surface of the sun and travel through space at about 250 mi/sec (400 km/sec). When they reach Earth's magnetosphere they cause a "bow shock" to form.

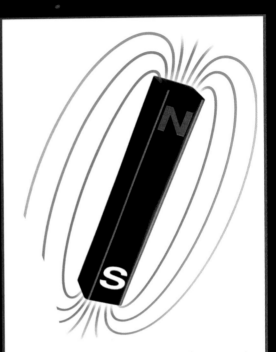

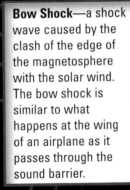

Bow Shock—a shock wave caused by the clash of the edge of the magnetosphere with the solar wind. The bow shock is similar to what happens at the wing of an airplane as it passes through the sound barrier.

Magnetosphere—the area around Earth that is affected by its magnetism. It is unevenly distributed about Earth, extending a distance equal to at least 10 times the width of the planet on the side farthest from the sun.

Solar Winds

Anyone who has ever used a magnetic compass to find their direction outdoors knows that there is a connection between our Earth and magnets. Back in 1600, a British doctor named William Gilbert proved that compasses work because our Earth itself behaves like a giant bar magnet with two magnetic poles near the true North and South poles. Originally, he thought that there was a giant magnet buried deep inside the Earth, but today, most scientists agree that the truth is far more complex.

Deep inside Earth, there are two different cores. The inner core is a solid mass of iron and nickel. It is surrounded by a molten outer core made up of liquid iron and nickel. As the world turns, these two cores spin at different rates. The difference in the motion in these two highly conductive cores generates an electrical current. Just like the spinning of electrons in atoms, this electrical current produces a magnetic field that affects the entire planet. This magnetic field not only is at work on the surface of the planet, but it extends thousands of miles into space. This area is called the magnetosphere.

Q & A

Smooth Operator

Now you know that the magnetosphere is the area of space around the planet that is generated by Earth's magnetic field. We sat down with Magneto, operator of the magnetosphere, for some insight into what goes on in his invisible magnetic bubble.

Q: For something no one can see, I'm surprised to hear that the magnetosphere has a lot of influence over Earth. Tell us about it.

A: Well, I'm not one to boast, but the planet would be a very different place if it weren't for the magnetosphere and the electromagnetic forces in it. In fact, if it weren't for electromagnetism, life as you know it would probably not even exist on Earth.

Q: That's a pretty big claim, Magneto.

A: And I do a pretty big job: operating a giant deflector shield to keep out the solar wind.

Q: Wait a minute. There's no air in space, so how can there be wind?

A: The solar wind isn't made up of moving air. It's a stream of electrically charged particles flowing out from the sun—flowing fast, I might add. The average speed is about a million miles (1,609,300 km) an hour.

Q: That's traveling, all right. In fact, at that speed the solar wind would reach Earth in about four days.

A: Right, if we let it in. But the magnetosphere makes sure it never reaches Earth. That's lucky for you because when those charged particles hit a planet, they can strip away the atmosphere. Some scientists think that's what happened to Earth's moon and to Mars: the solar wind did a number on them. Now they're just spinning chunks of rock. The magnetosphere tucks Earth inside a huge invisible blanket—that's thousands of miles thick in some places—in order to keep the solar wind out.

Q: Sounds like a lot of responsibility.

A: Oh, the pressure is unbelievable. And it's 24/7, no vacations, no calling in sick. After millions of years, let me tell you, it's wearing me down. The magnetosphere on the side of Earth facing the sun is thinner than the side facing away from it. It's been compressed by something called bow shock. But on the back of Earth, the magnetosphere stretches out about 100 times farther into a long magnetotail. Of course, you'll have to take my word for all of this because magnetism is a force, like gravity, and forces are invisible.

Q: Then how can we know things work the way you say they do?

A: It all depends on where you live. At the North and South Poles, the magnetosphere kind of bends in like a funnel. Some of the charged particles from the solar wind get into the upper atmosphere there. They interact with the sky and produce something called an aurora. In Alaska, they call it the Northern Lights. Sometimes when the sun is really pumping out energy, the auroras really kick up and people can see them half way around the equator! Most of the time, you have to be hanging out near Earth's poles to see an aurora.

Q: **So the magnetosphere originates at the top and bottom of the globe?**

A: Not at all. The magnetosphere comes from deep inside the planet, where Earth's liquid outer core sloshes around the solid inner core. Both of these cores are mostly made up of iron and nickel.

Q: **Hmmm. That's interesting because many magnets are made of iron and nickel, too.**

A: What, do you think that's a coincidence? Magnets are like miniature versions of Earth, each with its own north and south poles. It's also no coincidence that iron and nickel are both good conductors of electricity.

Q: **Hold on. I thought we were talking about magnetism, not electricity.**

A: You can't talk about one force without the other. The two are first cousins. Part and parcel. Two sides of the same coin. And so on. Electricity flowing through a conductor, such as copper wire, creates a magnetic field around the conductor. And a magnetic field and a conductor can produce an electric current. Both those things were demonstrated in experiments way back in the 1800s. That's what's going on in Earth's core all the time. As the planet spins, the metallic core generates electrical currents by something called a self-exciting dynamo. This dynamo effect creates the magnetism in the magnetosphere. It's hot stuff, and I mean that literally.

Q: **How hot?**

A: Scorching. Blazing. It's over 9,000 degrees Fahrenheit, which is 5,000 degrees Celsius in there. It needs to be that hot to keep the outer core liquid. The heat comes from pressure and all the radioactive elements concentrated in Earth's core. On Mars, the radioactive elements didn't last as long and things cooled off. Once the dynamo on Mars shut down, the magnetosphere became history. That meant the solar wind was free to come in and literally blow most of the Martian atmosphere away.

Q: **That's scary. Is there a chance that Earth's magnetosphere could disappear, too?**

A: Well, I suppose it's possible, but not anytime soon. Some scientists are concerned because the strength of Earth's magnetic field has decreased by as much as 15 percent since 1620. But the truth is that every time there's some kind of variation in the motion of Earth's core, the magnetosphere reacts. Earth's magnetic field always fluctuates in intensity. Over the last 75 million years or so, Earth's magnetic north and south poles have switched directions about 170 times. It's a big deal when it happens because for a short time the magnetosphere disappears, leaving Earth visible to solar wind. Once we get charged up again, though, we're ready for action.

Q: **That's a relief. You know, for something invisible, you're still very attractive.**

A: All magnets are. We can't help it. It just comes naturally. It's the way the electrons spinning in our atoms all line up in the same direction and produce magnetic domains. But thanks anyway. Well, I've got to go; there's too much activity going on in my layer to sit around and shoot the breeze for too long. And now...back to work.

Activity

MAYBE IT'S MAGNETIC Make a list of items to test with a magnet. Include nails, crushed multi-vitamins, silver, gold, and high-iron cereal. Predict which will have magnetic properties and explain why. Then, check their magnetic force by using a strong magnet and discuss the results.

Mad About Magnets

Although magnetism has only been strongly studied in the last few hundred years, magnets have been around for a long time. Their origin? The mighty lodestone. These iron ore rocks are made from magnetite, a natural mineral with magnetic properties. Lodestones were the first magnets people used. In 1269, Petris Peregrinis found that lodestone could transfer its magnetic power to an ordinary iron needle if rubbed against it long enough. He then found that if the needle rotated freely, it would always point in the same direction. Much to exploring sailors' delight, the modern-day compass was born. But there's more to the story...let the scrapbook be your guide.

Hwang-ti, Chinese Emperor, 2637 B.C

Rumor has it that this early Chinese Emperor knew about magnetism and used lodestones in his chariot. Ancient legends describe the figurine of a woman with an outstretched arm that would swivel at the front of his chariot and always point in the same direction, no matter which way the chariot faced. The key to this trick was that the Emperor concealed lodestones within the figurine, which caused it to be affected by Earth's magnetic field and always point in the same direction.

All Shook Up

Is it possible to demagnetize something? Sure. You can demagnetize a magnet by hitting it soundly with a hammer. The vibrations you cause when you strike the magnet will shake up the magnet's atoms and knock the domains out of alignment, so it will no longer be magnetic. To remagnetize it, you'll have to put it in touch with a magnetic field.

The First Compass

The Chinese were probably the first culture to recognize the direction-finding ability of magnets. In 83 A.D., during the Han dynasty, magnetic lodestone was carved into a bowl and spoon shape. The spoon was free to orient itself within the bowl to the direction of Earth's magnetic field, always pointing in the same direction. But it may not have been until 700 A.D. that magnetized metal needles were used in Chinese compasses as direction finders. By 1100 A.D., magnetized needles became common navigation instruments on ships across China. Knowledge about magnetism's direction-finding powers probably came to Europeans from the Chinese along the Silk Road, an overland trade route that connected the Far East with European cities. By 1270 A.D. compasses with floating, magnetized needles were common in Europe and considered a necessary instrument for navigation.

WOULD A MAGNET BY ANY OTHER NAME STILL BE SO ATTRACTIVE?

Lucretius, 100 B.C.

One possible origin for magnetism's name comes from Lucretius, a poet and naturalist who lived in ancient Rome. He recorded that the name "magnet" came from a place in the Greek province of Magnesia where lodestones were collected from the ground.

Pliny the Elder, 23–79 A.D.

But Pliny the Elder, a Roman naturalist, wrote in his book *Historia Naturalis* that the word for magnet comes from an old Greek shepherd named Magnes, "the nails of whose shoes and the tip of whose staff stuck fast in the magnetic field while he pastured his flocks." It appears that Magnes was herding his sheep in a field of lodestone.

Atlantic Ocean, October, 1492

Christopher Columbus reached the New World after a long and dangerous voyage across the Atlantic Ocean. Though Columbus took along a compass, he didn't trust it. Instead, on clear nights he would fix his position by celestial navigation—he found the moon more helpful than his compass. He was right in not letting the compass direct his ships. Columbus' compass was not giving him totally accurate information due to declination, which is the difference in position between the magnetic north pole and the geographic north pole. At the time that Columbus was sailing the Niña, the Pinta, and the Santa Maria, magnetic north was a little bit west of geographic north. That means that if he followed the compass, he would actually have been sailing a little bit south of west, when he thought he was sailing directly west.

Captain James Cook, Australia, 1770

During his explorations of the northeast coast of Australia, Captain James Cook wrote about an island in his captain's log, "I have given it the name Magnetical head or Isle as it had much the appearance of an Island and the compass would not travis it well when near it." Cook assumed the island was made mostly of lodestone, since it seemed to disturb his compass readings. Recent experiments show that the island is not magnetic, but it is still called Magnetic Island today.

Activity

MAKE YOUR OWN MAGNETISM SCRAPBOOK
See what sorts of far-out things you can discover about our magnetic universe. Look in magazines and newspapers and on the Internet for pictures and articles about people, places, things and events that involve, or are involved with magnetism. Cut the pictures out, collect clippings of the articles and make your own magnetism scrapbook or collage.

A Giant Step for Magnetkind

Way back in 1600, Queen Elizabeth I's physician, William Gilbert, proposed that compasses work because Earth itself is a giant magnet. To prove his theory, Gilbert rubbed a needle with lodestone, giving it magnetic properties. He stuck the needle in a cork and floated it in a water-filled goblet, so it could move freely. In test after test, the magnetized needle pointed down toward Earth. Gilbert's original theory was correct: Earth has a "magnetic soul."

Following are Gilbert's notes comparing Earth to that natural magnet, lodestone:

London, England, 1600

De Magnete by William Gilbert
Book I, Chapter XVII

To ward lodestone, as we see in the case of the Earth, magnetic bodies tend from all sides, and adhere to it; it has poles... natural points of force that through the co-operation of all its parts excel in prime efficiency; such poles exist also in the same way in the globe... . Like the Earth, it has an equator, a natural line of demarcation between the two poles... . Like the Earth, the lodestone has the power of direction and of standing still at north and south; it also has circular motion to the earth's position, whereby it adjusts itself to the earth's law... . The greater part of the visible earth is also magnetic, and has magnetic movements... .Thus every separate fragment of the earth exhibits in indubitable experiments the whole impetus of magnetic matter... .

Gilbert demonstrated that Earth must be magnetic by showing how a magnetized needle would dip at an angle to Earth's surface, just as a magnetized needle dips at angles to a spherical lodestone's surface.

MAGNETIC RECORDS

Almost 400 years after Gilbert's discovery, scientists are still learning about Earth's magnetism. They try to use observations as part of their evidence, just like Gilbert did. And as the geologists F.J. Vine and D.H. Matthews learned, one discovery about Earth often leads to another.

Have you ever looked at a map of the world as if it were a puzzle that needed putting together? Africa would fit nicely in the nook between North America and South America, just as the bulge on the top corner of South America would fit quite nicely in the curve of West Africa. People have long wondered why the continents seem to fit together so well. How could it be possible for these huge, lumbering masses of rock to ever move across the globe as easily as if they could float? It wasn't until the 1960s that scientists began to find evidence in Earth's magnetism suggesting that continents do float and drift across the globe and that at one time they fit together like a puzzle.

In 1963, Vine and Matthews were studying the sea floor. They knew that special machines called magnetic anomaly detectors (MADs), which are dragged behind boats over the Atlantic Ocean, revealed that rocks are magnetized in a banded, balanced pattern along the sea floor on either side of a mid-ocean ridge. Corresponding bands on either side of the ridge had been magnetized in different directions than the bands next to them. The scientists also knew that basalt (the rock that forms most of the sea floor and is rich in iron) is above the Curie point of temperature when it is molten. As the basalt cools and hardens, the iron in it becomes magnetized in the direction of Earth's magnetic field. The banding patterns on the ocean floor suggested that Earth has reversed its magnetic field many times through its history. But how could these patterns have formed?

Here's what F.J. Vine and D.H. Matthews figured out:

Mid-ocean ridges are actually cracks in the ocean's crust. As the continents are pushed apart by forces in Earth's mantle, pressure is released and molten rock flows up through the mid-ocean ridge cracks to fill the space left by the separation. This demonstrates that the ocean floor spreads. But not all scientists were convinced this new information also proved continents drifted. More evidence was needed.

This time the magnetic records on the continents helped provide the rest of the solution. Geologists who study the magnetic properties of igneous rocks noticed that they were magnetized in all different directions, not just north and south. As lava erupted from volcanoes and cooled into solid rock, iron in the rock was magnetized in the direction of the Earth's magnetic field at the time of the eruption. This "froze" the magnetic directions of north and south into the rock. Later, as the continents drifted, the rocks were turned in different directions so that their north and south alignment no longer matched the present day alignment on Earth. The only explanation for this was that the continents had somehow shifted in their position. The theory of continental drift gained much support.

Activity

POLAR PUZZLER Cut out pieces of paper or posterboard in the shapes of the continents. Arrange your continents on a piece of paper covering a flat surface just like they're arranged on a map of the world. Outline each continent in its current position, and then start puzzling. Experiment with how certain continental plates might have once fit together, and how they might have split up and "floated" into the positions they're in now.

Mind the Milestones

Ten discoveries in magnetism that have led to technological advances.

1

NAVIGATION, FIRST CENTURY AND EARLIER

By the year 83 A.D., Chinese mariners were using the direction-finding powers of magnetism to guide their travels. Yet, it wasn't until the 12th century, when knowledge of magnetism was passed along the Silk Road, that Western explorers really caught on to using compasses. Now we know that humans aren't the only animals that use Earth's magnetism for navigation. Whales, birds, lobsters, and even bacteria use it, too.

2

ELECTRIC MOTORS AND GENERATORS, 1820s–1830s

The work of Oersted and Faraday in the mid-1820s and 1830s led to the discovery that magnetism and electricity are closely related. Faraday used this knowledge to create the earliest generators and motors, revolutionizing technology and powering an electrical revolution around the world.

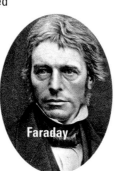
Faraday

3

ELECTROMAGNETIC WAVES, 1888

Heinrich Hertz discovered that electromagnetic waves can travel through space.

4

RADIO AND SATELLITE COMMUNICATION, 1911

Guglielmo Marconi used electromagnetism to transmit radio waves across the Atlantic Ocean. Electrical signals can be translated into electromagnetic waves that can then be transmitted across space as waves. When the electromagnetic waves are picked up by a receiver, they are once again translated into electrical signals and amplified into sound you can hear.

5

TELEVISION, 1920s

Since magnetism and electricity are related, magnets have an effect on electrons, whose flow creates electricity. Researchers used this knowledge to develop the technology in your television. One early version of the modern TV, called an iconoscope, was invented in 1923. Inside a TV, electrons are fired from an electron gun at the screen. They illuminate different colored particles that emit light when struck by electrons to create a color image. Electromagnets guide the stream of electrons to create images on the screen according to the radio signals received through the TV antenna.

Guglielmo Marconi

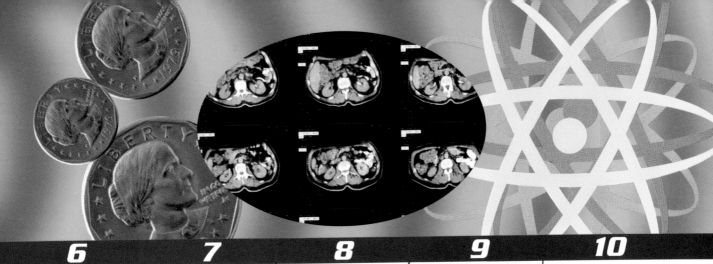

6 DATA STORAGE, 1950S

Without magnetism, computer diskettes would work better as drink coasters than as information holders. Without magnetism, you would be unable to record your favorite music on tape cassettes or save your homework on your computer. Once scientists learned about magnetic domains they could use magnets to store large amounts of information in small amounts of space. Mechanisms within computers, tape recorders, and stereos create magnetic patterns on magnetic surfaces so that information can be quickly condensed, stored, and then retrieved and read back.

7 CURRENCY/ FINANCES, 1950S

They say that money makes the world go round, but where would money be without magnetism? Ink that is used to print bank checks and currency is treated with magnetic dust so it can be distinguished from counterfeit currency. Vending machines and coin sorters use magnetism to determine real coins from fake ones, and to separate quarters from dimes and nickels.

8 TRAVEL, 1980S

Superconductors are metals that, when cooled to certain temperatures, show no resistance to the flow of electric current passing through because their atoms are too cold to vibrate. Magnetic levitating trains, or maglevs, make use of superconducting magnets to levitate or hover above their rails. They use magnetic repulsion and attraction to provide passengers with a smooth, fast ride, and give the environment a break by relying on the clean energy of magnetism instead of a fossil fuel.

9 MEDICINE, 1980S

Once scientists learned that magnetism was created by the motion of electrons around their nuclei, they knew in theory that anything could become a magnet if there was a force powerful enough to pull the paired electrons into alignment. Using superconducting magnets in magnetic resonance imaging machines, or MRIs, doctors have been able to induce magnetism in the atoms of patients. The MRI relies on an individual's patterns of magnetism to create images of their insides, helping doctors diagnose diseases such as cancer.

10 ENERGY PRODUCTION, 1990S

Huge Tokamak electromagnets are being used to attempt to harness the energy of atomic fusion in laboratories across the world and provide the energy of the future. If it becomes practical, atomic fusion will combine two hydrogen atoms to form one helium atom, producing a huge amount of energy in a process that will generate no pollution.

Activity

FUTURE FORCES Inventors, start your engines and peer into the future. Get together in a group and think about what the next technological advances based on magnetism might be. Brainstorm for ideas about how people could use magnetic energy, and come up with some inventions of your own. Compare your inventions with those of other groups in your class. Which inventions would be the most useful? Why? How could they be improved?

May the force be with you

Facts and figures about magnetism to keep at your fingertips

☞ If a bar magnet is broken in half, the two halves become two new magnets, each with a north and a south pole.

☞ Earth's magnetosphere extends 40,000 to 50,000 miles (60,000 to 80,000 km) into space on the side facing the Sun, and up to 186,500 miles (300,000 km) on the side away from the Sun. In some places, the magnetosphere reaches so far into space that the Moon passes through it in its orbit. The boundary where the magnetosphere ends is called the magnetopause.

☞ The Right-Hand Thumb Rule is an easy way of remembering the direction of a magnetic field that is produced by an electric current. If an electric current was flowing up through your right thumb, then the resulting magnetic field would go in the direction that your fingers curl.

☞ Solar wind is made up of charged particles speeding through space. When the solar wind collides with Earth's magnetosphere, the magnetic fields of the solar-wind particles and Earth's magnetosphere repel one another just like the same poles of two magnets. The side of the magnetosphere facing the Sun becomes compressed by the force of the solar wind and is called the "bow shock," while the side away from the Sun becomes drawn out into space and is called the "magnetotail."

☞ Since similar poles repel, the N pole on a compass needle or a magnet isn't really a magnetic north pole, but rather a north-seeking pole (or south pole) because it is attracted to Earth's magnetic north pole.

☞ Earth's magnetic field has a vertical component called inclination, which gets steeper the closer one gets to each magnetic pole. In 1831, James Clark Ross used magnetic inclination to discover the magnetic north pole. He had a special compass with a needle that could pivot both horizontally and vertically, and when his compass needle was pointing straight down, Ross knew that he had reached the magnetic north pole.

Polar Reversals

Earth's magnetic field flip-flops on average once every 500,000 years. Based on the various spread rates of the different ocean floor spreading zones, geologists figure that Earth's magnetic field has reversed about 171 times in the past 76 million years! Scientists aren't sure whether Earth's magnetic field decreases to zero and then builds back up again in the other direction, or if it simply flips direction. Scientists have noticed a scary relationship between polar reversals and large animal and plant extinctions. The reason could be that more harmful rays from the solar wind reach Earth when the magnetic field is near zero. But this explanation seems unlikely since most cosmic rays are absorbed by the atmosphere, rather than the magnetosphere. For now, the true answer remains unknown.

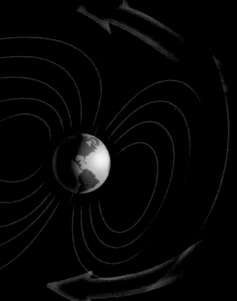

Magnetic Units

The strength of a magnetic field is measured in a unit called a gauss, which is named after the German mathematician Carl Friedrich Gauss (1777-1855). The strength of Earth's magnetic field at the surface is about 0.5 gauss. Ten thousand gauss is called a Tesla. The strongest magnets in the world are pulse magnets, which can produce magnetic fields of nearly 1,000 Teslas for periods that last a few millionths of a second. That's a magnetic field almost 20 million times more powerful than Earth's!

Separated at Birth?

We know that electricity and magnetism are very closely related because a Danish scientist named Hans Christian Oersted discovered in 1820 that electric current, or the flow of electrons, can produce a magnetic field. Then, in 1831, an English scientist named Michael Faraday discovered that the movement of a magnetic field can also produce an electric current, proving that one cannot exist without the other.

Curie Point

French scientist Pierre Curie (1859-1906) discovered that when magnets are heated beyond a certain temperature they lose their magnetic properties. As a magnet is heated, its molecules begin to vibrate faster and faster. Finally, they reach a point when they lose their alignment and the magnetic domains become randomly arranged, so the magnet loses its magnetism. This temperature is known as the Curie point in honor of Pierre Curie. The Curie point for magnetite is about 500 °C.

A Shocking

At an assembly of the Royal Society of London today, Mr. Michael Faraday presented an electrifying account of his research building on Hans Christian Oersted's 1820 discovery that magnetism and electricity are related.

Mr. Faraday found that an electric current produces a magnetic field—and consequently, that electricity can produce mechanical action—when he set up a wire to move around a current-carrying conductor. But he didn't stop there. He also conceived of a way to produce the opposite effect—converting the mechanical movements of magnets into electricity.

Indeed, these current findings are very attractive, and it is quite possible that they will lay the foundation for a new age of electricity.

Excerpts from Faraday's diary detailing the experiment that led to the first electric motor:

August 29, 1831

1. *Experiments on production of electricity from magnetism.*

2. *Have had an iron ring made (soft iron), iron round and 7/8-inches thick and ring 6 inches in external diameter. Wound many coils of copper wire round one half, the coils*

The dynamo invented by Michael Farada[y] in 1831.

Discovery

being separated by twine and calico—there were three lengths of wire, each about 24-feet long, and they could be connected as one length or used as separate lengths … Will call this side of the ring 'A.' On the other side, separated by an interval, was wound wire in two pieces together amounting to about 60 feet in length, the direction being as with the former coils … this side call 'B.'

3. Charged a battery of 10 plates 4 inches square. Made the coil on B side one coil and connected its extremities by a copper wire passing to a distance and just over a magnetic needle (3 feet from iron ring). Then connected the ends of one of the pieces on A side with battery; immediately a sensible effect on needle. It oscillated and settled at last in original position. On breaking connection of A side with battery again a disturbance of the needle.

4. Made all the wires on A side one coil and sent current from battery through the whole. Effect on needle much stronger than before.

Activity

GENERATING EXCITEMENT In 1831, Michael Faraday built the first electric generator with a copper disc that spun in a magnetic field. This device produced a continuous electric current or direct current (DC). Generators can also produce currents that change direction, or alternating currents (ACs). AC currents drive most household appliances. Now it's your turn to convert mechanical energy into electrical energy by making your own AC electric generator.

What you'll need:
- 2 pieces of insulated copper wire about 25 feet (8m) long
- a tall, thin glass or bottle
- wire stripper or craft knife
- cardboard toilet paper tube
- masking tape
- compass
- bar magnet

What you'll do:
1. Remove 1 inch (2.5cm) of insulation from both ends of both pieces of wire.
2. Tightly wrap one wire around the bottle 40 times, leaving about 1 foot (30cm) of wire free at each end. Tape the coil of wire to the bottle to keep it in place. This is a solenoid.
3. Lay the compass inside the solenoid to act as your current detector, or galvanometer.
4. Make another solenoid by wrapping the second piece of wire around the cardboard tube. Make sure the ends of the wire extend outward 2.5 to 3 feet (0.8 to 0.9m).
5. Attach one end of the wire from the galvanometer to one end of the wire from the second solenoid. Attach the other end of the galvanometer wire to the other end of the solenoid wire, making a complete circuit. Hold the second solenoid away from the galvanometer.
6. Slide the bar magnet into the middle of the cardboard tube, then pull it back out. What happens to the compass needle in the galvanometer? Keep sliding the magnet in and out of the tube and watch what happens. You're generating an electric current with the motion of a magnet!

Think about these:
1. Why does the solenoid with the compass have to be placed far away from the solenoid with the magnet in order to detect an electrical current?
2. Why does the needle on the compass deflect one way when you push the magnet in the tube, and the other way when you pull it out?

Magnets Do the Darndest Things

The first technological use of magnetism was probably the magnetic compass. Today, magnetism and electromagnetism (magnetism induced by an electric current) are the driving forces in devices we use every day. When you pick up the telephone to talk to a friend, the incoming electrical signal passes through an electromagnet that attracts a thin iron disc, or diaphragm, with varying signal strengths. The vibrations of the diaphragm pass through the air as sound waves, and you hear them as speech.

Magnets are also used in doorbells, surgical tools, radios and hundreds of other things. **See if you can match the pictures on the right with the descriptions of how magnets make them work.**

A. (doorbell)

B. (refrigerator door)

C. (cassette tape)

D. (electric motor inside a fan)

E. (computer disc

F. (alarm)

G. (jukebox or vending machine)

H. (speakers)

I. (television)

1. A current feeds into a coil positioned between the poles of a permanent magnet. The interaction between the magnetic fields of the coil and the permanent magnet causes the coil to turn. On every half-turn, the current reverses to keep the coil rotating.

2. Electrical signals are translated into electron beams, which are guided by electromagnets across the back of a screen. Varying currents in the electromagnetic coils produce changing magnetic fields. These fields then deflect the electron beams across and down the screen, where they strike different chemicals to create a color picture.

3. Electrical signals pass through a wire coil on a cone-shaped electromagnet. A strong permanent magnet is nearby, and when the current flows one way, magnetic force pushes the cone outward. When the current flows in the opposite direction, the cone is pulled inward. The vibrations of the cone's movement form sound waves that are sent through the air.

4. A current flows through a solenoid (long wire wound into a tightly cylindrical coil), and its magnetic field attracts an iron bar connected to a hammer. When the iron bar moves, the hammer strikes a bell.

5. A coin passing through a magnetic field is slowed down. If the coin is non-metallic, it won't slow down, and will be channeled into a reject chute. If the coin is made of the wrong metal, it may slow too much; again, the reject chute. The correct coin will slow down just enough to pass over the reject chute and continue into the next part of the machine.

6. When the building is secure, a magnetic circuit between the door and its frame is closed. But when the door is opened, the electronically monitored circuit is broken, triggering a not-so-welcoming sound.

7. This device stores data and information as magnetic patterns on a flat disc, which are converted from electrical signals.

8. Magnetic patterns are applied to a thin coat of iron or chromium metal. The patterns are read by an electromagnet, converted into electrical signals, and reproduced as sound.

9. Magnetic particles imbedded in rubber make a seal very attractive, and help this device keep its cool.

Answers: 1. D; 2. I; 3. H; 4. A; 5. G; 6. F; 7. E; 8. C; 9. B.

Activity

A DAY WITHOUT MAGNETS You wake up hungry with breakfast on your mind. You pour yourself a bowl of cereal and then head to the refrigerator to get some milk. Hmmm. There are magnets on the floor and the refrigerator door is hanging open. What is going on?

Write a journal entry for a typical day—but a day without magnets. How do you use magnets in your daily life, and how would things be different for you on a day without magnets?

Keep It Up!

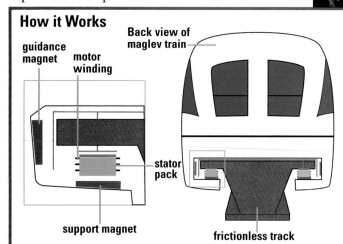

Magicians trick their audiences into thinking they can levitate people. But science, not trickery, is involved in levitating an entire train. Magnetic levitation (maglev) trains are supported by powerful magnetic fields, so they "float" above frictionless tracks because of magnetism.

There are two primary types of maglevs, and they both use magnetic attraction and repulsion to move faster and smoother than electric trains. Both maglevs have rails that contain electromagnets attached to the bottom sides of the track. The sides of the train wrap around these rails and electromagnets on the bottom of the vehicle pull toward the electromagnets in the rails, causing the train to stay properly aligned through attractive forces. While the two models are very similar, there are some important differences.

One design, currently being used on a 4-mile (7 km) test track in Miyazaki, Japan, makes use of the opposing force between superconducting magnets on the train and electrically conductive strips on the track. This electrodynamic suspension (EDS) system is considered the most stable because it does not require continued adjustment. However, superconducting magnets are more expensive than conventional ones, which are used in the other kind of maglev also, and this system requires a refrigeration set-up in the train to keep the magnets at cool temperatures.

The other kind of maglev system is called electromagnetic suspension (EMS). Its train bottom uses conventional electromagnets that are fitted at the ends of two structures under the train, which wrap around both sides of it. The train is pulled upward toward the iron rails of the track, lifting the train so that it hovers about 4–6 inches (10–15 cm) above it. This system is currently being tested on a 19.6 mile (31.5 km) track in Emsland, Germany.

Magnetism also propels these maglev trains. Magnetic fields in the track interact with magnetic fields in the vehicle, alternating attraction and repulsion to move the hovering maglev forward. A linear induction motor (LIM) creates an electric current from these changing magnetic fields, thrusting the maglev straight ahead.

A maglev train ride is smooth and quiet because by varying the current supplied to the motors, the train can change its speed much more smoothly than if it relied on gears. Also, because there's little friction between the track and wheels, maglev trains can go really fast—more than 300 miles (483 km) per hour. In fact, on April 14, 1999, a manned maglev train in Japan reached a speed of 342 mph(550 kmph)!

Besides Germany and Japan, maglevs are currently in use at Disney World in Florida. They are being developed for use elsewhere in Europe, the United States and other parts of the world. In fact, the German Parliament has recently approved plans for a 175 mile (282 km) maglev route from Berlin to Hamburg, but it's not expected to be up until 2005.

How it Works

guidance magnet

motor winding

Back view of maglev train

stator pack

support magnet

frictionless track

Activity

DESTINATION VACATION If maglev trains are pressed into service along convenient routes, how long will it take to get from your home to your favorite spots? Consult a map and mileage chart to figure out where you would go on a maglev train and how long it would take you to get there. Where should they be placed around the country in order to serve the most people?

AT THE Speed OF THE Sun

It's hot—as much as 115,000 times hotter than boiling water. No number of fans or amount of air conditioning is gonna help here. Even atoms can't hold themselves together.

And here you are, swimming around in the thin, gassy soup of the Sun's broken-up atoms, holding onto an electron for dear life. You pass through a sun spot, a relatively cooler, darker spot.

But the sun spot is like a magnetic storm, and it's disturbing the magnetic fields on the surface of the Sun, causing strange things to happen. What's this?! Ack! It's a solar flare—an arc of burning gases suspended by magnetism, and induced by the magnetic activity of multiplying sun spots. It's bursting from the surface like a giant flaming tongue the size of 12 Earths, and you're on it. Hold on—you're in for the ride of your life!

The charged particles—protons, electrons, and neutrons from super-heated atoms—that have escaped from the Sun and are traveling outward into space, are called the solar wind. But this is no

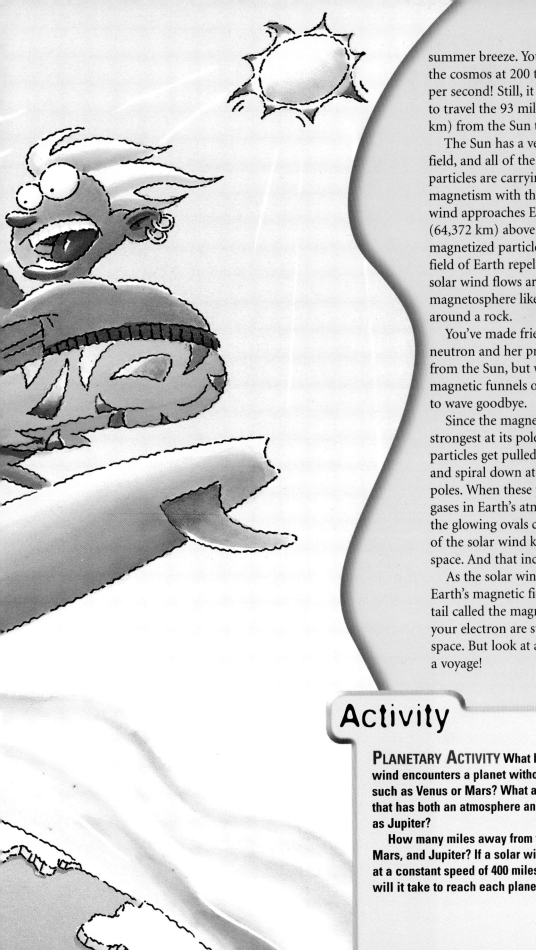

summer breeze. You're hurtling through the cosmos at 200 to 500 miles (805 km) per second! Still, it takes about four days to travel the 93 million miles (150 million km) from the Sun to Earth.

The Sun has a very powerful magnetic field, and all of the charged solar-wind particles are carrying a little bit of that magnetism with them. When the solar wind approaches Earth 40,000 miles (64,372 km) above its surface, the magnetized particles and the magnetic field of Earth repel each other, and the solar wind flows around Earth's magnetosphere like a stream flowing around a rock.

You've made friends with a nifty neutron and her proton pal on your trip from the Sun, but when you pass by the magnetic funnels of Earth's poles, it's time to wave goodbye.

Since the magnetic pull of Earth is strongest at its poles, some solar-wind particles get pulled into the magnetic field and spiral down at the north and south poles. When these particles collide with gases in Earth's atmosphere, they create the glowing ovals called auroras. But most of the solar wind keeps going out into space. And that includes you.

As the solar wind streams by, it draws Earth's magnetic field out into a cometlike tail called the magnetotail. Now you and your electron are surfing off into deeper space. But look at all you've done! What a voyage!

Activity

PLANETARY ACTIVITY What happens when the solar wind encounters a planet without a magnetic field, such as Venus or Mars? What about another planet that has both an atmosphere and a magnetic field, such as Jupiter?

How many miles away from the Sun are Venus, Mars, and Jupiter? If a solar wind particle is traveling at a constant speed of 400 miles per second, how long will it take to reach each planet?

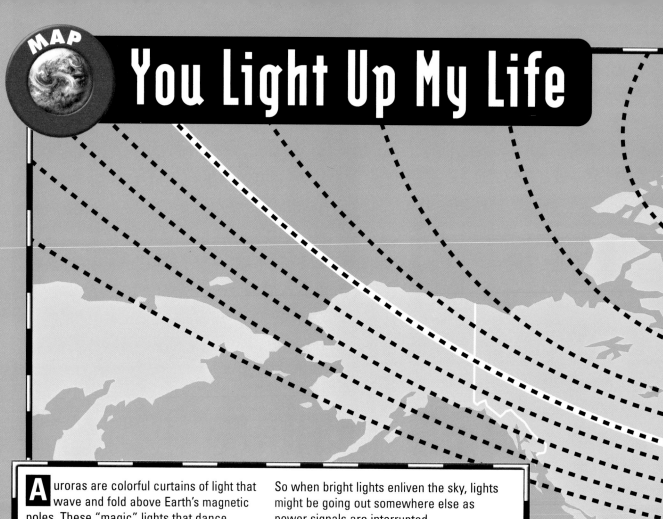

You Light Up My Life

Auroras are colorful curtains of light that wave and fold above Earth's magnetic poles. These "magic" lights that dance across the night sky are created by charged particles flying from the Sun's surface and colliding with gases in Earth's atmosphere.

The particles speed outward from the Sun in a flow called the solar wind. When the solar wind approaches Earth, most of it is deflected by our planet's magnetosphere. But some particles are funneled down through the atmosphere at the North and South Poles, where Earth's magnetic attraction is strongest.

When these particles hit gases in the atmosphere, such as oxygen, nitrogen, helium, argon, neon and mercury, the atoms become "excited" and give off light. Down here on Earth, we see this light as the Northern Lights, or Aurora Borealis, and the Southern Lights, or Aurora Australis. From space, auroras look like bright ovals surrounding the north and south poles.

Auroras can be beautiful, but they can also be warning signs of major magnetic disturbances, or magnetic storms, on Earth.

So when bright lights enliven the sky, lights might be going out somewhere else as power signals are interrupted, communication systems fail and satellites in orbit are damaged by solar wind particles.

This map shows aurora-observation bands in the north, which are determined by aurora sightings. By looking at the map, you will find that if you live in Fairbanks, Alaska, you have about an 85 percent chance of seeing the Northern Lights, but your chances decrease as you move farther away from Earth's magnetic north pole. Your chances of seeing the lights also decrease if you move north past the peak of the auroral zone, or the 100 percent band. This happens because you've moved inside the aurora oval that surrounds the magnetic north pole.

Northern Lights, or Aurora Borealis

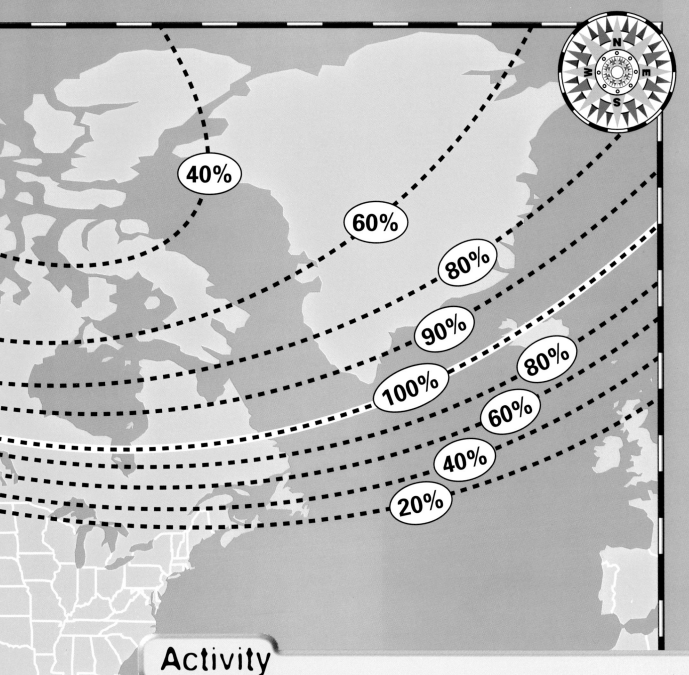

Activity

OGLING AURORAS Have you ever seen the Northern Lights? What are your chances?

Locate the places on the right on the map and see where they fall within aurora-observation belts. Do some searching of your own and plot a city or landmark that isn't on the list in each observation belt. Where would you go for your next aurora-sighting vacation?

PLACES:

Bathurst Island, Canada

Minneapolis, Minnesota

Point Barrow, Alaska

Montreal, Canada

Reykjavík, Iceland

Nuuk, Greenland

Nord, Greenland

Nome, Alaska

Calgary, Alberta

Newfoundland

Saskatoon, Saskatchewan

Belcher Island

Hebrides (in Great Britain)

Bottineau, North Dakota

Caribou, Maine

Anadyr, Siberia

The Problem with Pigeons

Magnetically Inclined

Every spring and autumn, hundreds of thousands of birds set off on a long, hard migration to their summer or winter homes. Many birds migrate to follow the food supply as the seasons change. Warmer weather usually means more food, and for many birds in the northern hemisphere, heading south for the winter becomes a necessity for survival.

How is it that many animals are able to successfully "navigate" through unknown territory for the first time to reach a final destination they may have never seen before? Are they born knowing in which direction to fly?

As it turns out, the answer is a little more complicated than that. Check out the clues below, then read the story on the opposite page and see if you can answer the questions about the birds that couldn't find their way home.

▶ Magnetite is a mineral made from iron that is very sensitive to magnetism. It is found in very small quantities in the brains of many different species of animals, including humans.

▶ Some bacteria are able to produce magnetite from iron they ingest in the soil.

▶ Small magnets that are more powerful than Earth's magnetic field can influence magnetically sensitive materials if they are close by. For example, a compass needle will normally point to Earth's North Pole. But when a bar magnet is brought near it, the compass needle will point in the direction of the bar magnet's north pole instead.

▶ Pigeons are able to navigate using different environmental cues. One environmental cue that they use to navigate is the Sun, but they have to be able to see it in the sky to navigate with it.

The Problem with the Pigeons

You have been asked to serve as a research assistant to a respected scientist, Dr. Hazel Birdsnoggin, on her most recent scientific expedition. Her mission is to solve, once and for all, the question of whether birds actually use Earth's magnetic field to migrate. Gathering your gear and the scientist's equipment, which includes a few dozen caged pigeons, you head out for the field.

After hiking due south through swamp, thickets, forest and brush, you reach the remote expedition site, which is a treeless hill located several miles from any disturbances that might affect experimental results. You quickly set up the mobile laboratory unit, and begin the initial preparations. While unpacking the scientist's gear, you find several small magnets attached to what appear to be mini chinstraps. Dr. Birdsnoggin informs you that they are magnet-helmets, specially designed to fit snugly on the pigeons' heads. You prepare your notebook and instruments for the next day's experiment. Then, exhausted from your long hike, you drift off into a deep sleep counting pigeons.

The next day is perfectly clear and sunny, and Dr. Birdsnoggin wakes you up for her first round of experiments. The first group of pigeons is brought to the hilltop. Five of the pigeons, none of which is wearing a helmet, are released from their cages one by one. Each pigeon flies north, which is the direction of their roost back at the doctor's lab. Using a compass, you note the flight direction of each of the birds as they are released.

Five more pigeons are released, and this time each pigeon has a magnet strapped to its head. You note in your journal that each pigeon flies directly north, the exact direction of the roost. The scientist is pleased, and you return to camp to prepare for the next round of experiments, which requires a cloudy and overcast day.

When you awake, you notice that the weather is in your favor. There isn't a single patch of blue in the sky. You trek up the hilltop with another batch of pigeons. The first five pigeons are released without magnets and you record the direction of their flight—due north, once again. The next five pigeons are released, and this last group of pigeons have magnets strapped to their heads. As the first pigeon flutters into the air, you prepare to write what you have recorded every time since these experiments began—north—only this time the pigeons do something different. They fly in all different directions across the sky—southeast, west, northwest, southwest—and each pigeon, stalled by apparent confusion, finally gives up and lands a short distance away from where it took off.

Dr. Birdsnoggin pats you on the back in triumph and strides off down the hill to collect the lost and confused pigeons. As you pack up the mobile lab and begin the long march back, you begin to think about the results of the expedition's experiments.

Questions

1. Why would Dr. Birdsnoggin want to strap magnets on the pigeons' heads?

2. What are some of the man-made things that couldn't be present in the testing area for this experiment to work? (Hint: It's really quite shocking.)

3. How were the pigeons that were released on a cloudy day without magnets able to find their way home?

4. If the pigeons used magnetism to navigate, how were the pigeons released on a sunny day able to find their way home even though they had magnets on their heads?

5. Why did the experiments have to be done on a sunny day and on a cloudy day?

6. What mineral might a scientist expect to find if she dissected a pigeon's brain tissue?

Answer is on inside back cover.

Energy to Burn

"Mr. Magnet" helps kids see the super-powers of energy.

Imagine a world with no pollution, where all the energy we produce is as clean as water and light. There will be no more dirty coal-burning electricity plants bellowing black clouds that cause acid rain, which strips away living layers of earth. We will no longer worry about fossil fuels releasing carbon dioxide into the atmosphere and increasing the greenhouse effect, which causes global warming. Nuclear fission reactors that split atoms of uranium to create energy, as well as dangerous and highly radioactive waste, will be a thing of the past. People will no longer risk depleting the world's energy stores of coal, natural gas, and oil—all thanks to the power of magnets.

"Magnets make the world go," says Paul Thomas, an engineer at the Massachusetts Institute of Technology. His life-long fascination with magnets has earned him a nickname, and as "Mr. Magnet," Thomas teaches kids across the Northeast about magnetism. "Magnetism is a fundamental force of nature—it's like gravity, and can do very neat things like confining plasmas (in fusion reactors). You can find magnets everywhere— they're in electronic toothbrushes and TVs. Life without magnets would be life without electricity— you wouldn't be able to listen to the radio and the school bus wouldn't work."

When he isn't teaching, Thomas is working at MIT's plasma fusion center to build a new type of reactor called a levitating dipole reactor (LDR). He plans to make nuclear fusion a practical reality, and he is using one of the world's most sophisticated magnets to do it. If he gets his way, future power plants will produce energy using magnets and hydrogen, the most abundant element in the universe and the same fuel the Sun uses to heat our solar system.

Nuclear fusion is the opposite of nuclear fission, which splits atoms apart. Nuclear fusion is the process of combining atomic nuclei to form new and bigger atoms. Fusion and fission may sound similar, but when it comes to producing energy, they are worlds apart. Both reactions convert mass into energy following Albert Einstein's famous equation, $E=mc^2$. But nuclear fission pollutes with radioactive waste, while nuclear fusion produces only helium, a naturally occurring atmospheric gas.

In $E=mc^2$, E stands for the amount of energy released, which is equal to m—the difference between mass at the end of the reaction and the beginning of a reaction—multiplied by c^2—a number that stands for the speed of light (186,000 miles per second) times itself. One thing this equation demonstrates is that a very small difference in mass can produce a huge amount of energy. This fact forms the basis for nuclear fusion power.

Fusion reactions don't happen naturally on Earth because hydrogen atoms have the same charge, and similar charges repel. To get hydrogen atoms together, scientists must use huge amounts of energy—enough to power a small city. Since heat is

Einstein's energy equation is helpful in putting together modern energy solutions.

a good source of energy, scientists heat hydrogen atoms to temperatures of about 50 million degrees Fahrenheit. That's about twice as hot as the center of the Sun! But nothing on Earth can withstand temperatures above one million degrees Fahrenheit. This is where magnets comes in to play.

Super-heated hydrogen gas becomes a plasma, a collection of protons and electrons that conducts electricity and is affected by magnetism. As the hydrogen heats up, a powerful doughnut-shaped magnet called a Tokamak in the LDR squeezes the fiery plasma away from the walls of the reactor. It's like an invisible bottle created by magnetic force. Since the plasma is contained within this "bottle," and never touches the relatively cool reactor walls, it can reach high temperatures without melting the reactor. Once the temperature is hot enough, hydrogen atoms fuse and energy is given off.

Things that run on electricity and fossil fuels now, may run on fusion energy in the future. "Maybe within the next 50 years we'll see fusion power," Thomas says. "And if it replaces fossil fuel burning, that is going to reduce emissions and maybe slow down global warming."

Right now the plasma reactor requires more energy than it produces, but research is producing promising results. Once the secret to affordable nuclear fusion is solved and the process is made practical, hydrogen atoms from a few gallons of sea water could power an entire city without a puff of pollution. That's why Mr. Magnet and other researchers around the world are hoping that magnets will help power the world with clean energy— something we could all use.

Are you drawn to the magnetic field?

"Understanding magnetism and being able to create it at will proved to be fundamental to setting the scene for the creation of our modern world," wrote magnetician Gerrit Verschuur in 1993. Where will magnetism lead you in the future?

The best step to achieving a career in magnetism is by earning a college degree in one of many fields of study, such as geology, physics, engineering, materials science, math, and even biology. Some students of magnetism continue their education to earn a master's degree or a Ph.D. But for now, junior high and high school science and math classes, as well as computer and writing classes, will help prepare you to research magnetism and think of new ways to use magnets. Once the school work is done, you will be able to apply your knowledge and make a difference in your community.

Perhaps you'll study biology and research how biomagnetism can affect animal behavior. Or maybe you'll become a doctor, nurse, or medical technician and work with MRI machines, helping save lives by diagnosing cancer and other deadly diseases in patients who can still be treated.

If geology captures your imagination, you might teach how Earth's magnetic record is preserved in rocks, or discover the secrets of Earth's magnetic field. Maybe you will be the one to predict, and even help reverse, the depletion of Earth's magnetosphere, saving the entire planet. Or will you explore Mars with other astronauts in search of answers to the red planet's magnetic history?

If you become a materials scientist, you'll help make our lives easier by inventing devices that rely on magnetism. As a physicist or an engineer, you can take your inventiveness a few steps farther and devise new applications for magnets that may help make our world, and our universe, a better place to live.

LEGENDARY LIGHTS

In Finland long ago, people thought that foxes with bright, sparkling fur were running and playing in the mountains of Lapland, an area that is north of Finland in the Arctic Circle. Since they attributed the colorful Northern Lights to these playful foxes, the Finns called aurora activity "fox fires."

The Athabaskan people of Alaska believed that the spirits of tribal members who had died watched protectively over those still living. They saw the Aurora Borealis as evidence of these "sky dwellers" communicating with their loved ones.

Way up north on Saint Lawrence Island in Canada, the Yupik people say that the Northern Lights used to be colorless. Yupik children were warned not to go outside at night or the lights would take them away. But some children didn't listen, and they were stolen by the lights. So now the lights have colors—the bright parkas of the stolen children dancing across the sky.

Seeing Spots

The Chinese may have been the first to notice dark spots on the Sun more than 2,000 years ago, but it wasn't until recently that scientists discovered that these sunspots are really magnetic disturbances on the surface of the Sun. Heat traveling from the Sun's center to its surface is slowed down near sunspots because the spots' magnetic fields deflect the flow of heat from the Sun's core. Sunspots appear dark because they are relatively cool areas on the Sun's red-hot surface.

Macho Magnet

The Tokamak is a super magnet at MIT's plasma fusion lab that is so powerful that it could lift a stack of Volkswagens as tall as Mt. Everest—that's 25,000,000 pounds (11,340,000 kg) of force!

Are you in the loop?

The Sun goes through cycles of about 11 years each when it is "active" and "quiet." During an active Sun, sunspots multiply, causing solar flares to erupt and send hundreds of millions of tons of solar-wind particles hurtling through space. With this overload of particles in Earth's atmosphere, auroral ovals can stretch beyond where they're normally seen. Someone as far south as Mississippi might see the northern lights during a really active sun cycle, while someone in Alaska or Northern Canada, where the lights can normally be seen, won't be able to, because he or she is inside the auroral oval.

Word Wise

▶ The word "lodestone" comes from the Middle English word "lode," meaning "to lead."

▶ Aurora (the Roman goddess of dawn), was the name given to the Northern Lights by Pierre Gassendi in 1621. He added "Borealis" to refer to the Roman god of the north wind, whose name is Boreas. Captain James Cook named the Southern Lights the Aurora Australis, or "southern dawn" in 1773, when he was sailing near Antarctica.

Lobster Metalheads!

Bacteria and Dr. Birdsnoggin's pigeons aren't the only organisms that use magnetism to navigate. Spiny lobsters know which way to go thanks to their internal compass. In late autumn the lobsters move to warmer water in preparation for a chilly winter. Amazingly they reach their destination through the dark of night and huge waves every year without fail. How? They've got tiny bits of magnetite—the same material that's in lodestones—in their brains! The lobsters' migration is guided by their detection of Earth's magnetic field.

Seeing Red

Jupiter, which has both an atmosphere and a magnetosphere, has auroral ovals over each of its magnetic poles. But since Jupiter's atmosphere is largely made up of hydrogen (unlike Earth's, which is mostly oxygen and nitrogen), dark red is the color produced when solar wind particles collide with atmospheric gases to make the auroras.

Mesmerizing Material

Have you ever been mesmerized by something or someone? The word "mesmerize" actually comes from a man named Franz Anton Mesmer, who in the 1700s claimed to be able to heal people by manipulating magnets and using "mesmerism," or hypnotic powers. Acclaimed by some as a miraculous healer and by others as a fantastic fraud, Mesmer theorized that a very subtle magnetic force flowed between everything. Although his healing powers may have been more fake than fact, he wasn't entirely off base. Everything does have atoms, and atoms have electricity, which produces magnetism. Most of the time, however, the spin of atoms' electrons cancel each other out, so not everything is actually magnetic.

Magnetized Bacteria

The bacteria *Aquaspirillum magnetotacticum* has no eyes but still manages to find its way to its food source deep in the muck of salt water marshes. It uses Earth's magnetic field to guide its way. Scientists have discovered that members of this species have a tiny chain of magnetite inside their cell that they use to detect the direction of

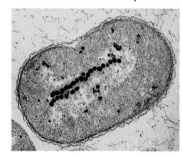

Earth's magnetic field. Not only do these bacteria know which direction is north, they can also use magnetic inclination to figure out which way is down—the direction of their food source!

MEDICAL MAGNETISM

From MRIs to surgical "tweezers" that pull magnetic objects out of people's bodies, magnetism is alive and well in the medical profession. There are many people who believe that magnets can also be used therapeutically to help our bodies heal, or at least feel less pain from such ailments as arthritis, chronic back pain, tennis elbow, and knee injuries.

Our blood contains iron. And according to some studies, more blood cells are drawn to a specific area when magnets are held over it, helping to stimulate blood circulation and accelerate the healing process. Other scientists believe that magnets can alleviate pain in some people because magnetic energy affects chemical interactions in nerve fibers that are responsible for pain impulses. The debate is ongoing about whether or not magnets can help heal you, but there is no evidence that magnets harm you. (Of course, you should keep magnets away from pacemakers, electrical implants, and any other medical device that could be affected by magnetic force.)

YOUR WORLD · YOUR TURN

Final Project:
Going, going, gone

You are the chief researcher in charge of a governmental agency devoted to the study of magnetism. The agency's commission is to report any findings concerning the status of Earth's magnetic field directly to the president of the United States.

Recently, one of your leading teams of highly trained geophysicists has brought to your attention the startling news that Earth's magnetic field is rapidly diminishing at a rate that will bring the field to zero within the next year. Of course, this is an extremely troubling development, and so far, the cause of the depletion is unknown.

Your agency's task is immediately focused on what will happen to Earth when the magnetic field reaches zero. The geophysicists believe that there are two possible scenarios:

One: Earth's magnetic field will reach zero, the magnetic poles will reverse, and the magnetic field will immediately return again, only in the opposite direction.

Two: Earth's magnetic field will reach zero and stay there because Earth's self-exciting dynamo has finally burned itself out.

It's your job to tell the president about this impending disaster, backing up your news with the most accurate information on the matter, and to give advice to the president on what to do. The government is depending on your information and advice so that it can act swiftly to control the situation before it gets out of hand, maintain order within the country, and hopefully prevent a worldwide crisis.

Gather friends or teammates around and answer these questions:

1 What are the possible dangers of reversed polarity and a zero magnetic field? How would a reduced magnetic field affect Earth's magnetosphere? What would happen to the magnetosphere if the field reversed?

2 How should the president prepare the country for each of the possible scenarios? What major industries and infrastructure systems might be especially affected by the predicted magnetic depletion?

3 Based on your knowledge of Earth's interior and how it generates its magnetic field, can you think of anything that can be done to prevent the depletion of Earth's magnetism should such a crisis occur?

4 Using what you know about magnetism and electricity, design an invention that might create an artificial magnetic field to take the place of Earth's should it ever fail. What are the difficulties involved in creating such a device? Are there any special considerations you must take into account?

Ready for the ultimate challenge?
Enter this or any other science project in the Discovery Young Scientist Challenge.
Visit discoveryschool.com/dysc to find out how.